To Kari

Thank you for serving.

Alicia

THANK **YOU**
for serving in children's ministry!

THIS IS A GIFT OF THANKS FOR:

HEARTFELT THANKS FOR SERVING IN CHILDREN'S MINISTRY

Visit our website: **group.com**

Created by the amazing team at Group Publishing. Thanks, team! You're awesome!

ISBN 978-14707-3221-9

10 9 8 7 6 5 4 3 2 1   20 19 18 17 16 15

Printed in the United States of America.

INTRODUCTION

It may be something as simple as a smile or a hug at just the right moment. Or perhaps it's something a little more involved—a specially prepared meal that teaches about people in other lands…a song or Scripture that simply sticks…the gift of a new Bible. Whatever that small but meaningful gesture is, it leaves a lasting impression on a child. An impression that makes a difference.

As a Sunday school teacher or ministry leader or children's volunteer, you have that impact on children. Your smile, your time, your caring words, your guidance, your high fives—they add up to the sharing of God's love. And they make a difference.

Tucked in this book you'll find stories of lives that were changed by someone just like you—plus you'll find devotions, Bible verses, and quotes that will encourage your heart and remind you that what you do touches the heart of a child and can have eternal impact.

**THANK YOU FOR SERVING IN CHILDREN'S MINISTRY.
YOU DO MAKE A DIFFERENCE.**

LOVE IN AN ENVELOPE

Timidly I walked into the class of babies and toddlers. We were new to the church, and I was a little nervous taking our kids to a class of strangers. A woman with a huge smile met us and asked my son's name. She swooped him up in her welcoming arms and took him over to join the other children in their activity. I was a little taken aback by her friendliness—it was almost too much for me, and I'm an outgoing person! But it wasn't long before "Mrs. Bonnie" was a highlight of our week. She became a dear friend to my young son, and he couldn't wait to see her. Bounding down the stairs of the church, he would throw himself into her arms and chatter happily about his life.

One day after church we invited Mrs. Bonnie and her husband Mr. Lewis over for lunch. Little by little, this dear woman wove her way into our hearts simply by loving our children. We moved away, but it didn't matter to Bonnie. For 15 years she has faithfully sent birthday cards to every member of our family. Each one has a word of Christ-like encouragement and love.

The cool thing is that we are not the only family who has been the recipient of Bonnie's love and kindness. She has a full-time ministry of sending cards out to nearly 100 people a month...people who have been touched by the love of Jesus—in the form of a card inside an envelope.

Bonnie has watched kids grow from toddlers to teens, from babies to brides. She calls on occasion just to check in on "her boys." There's not a thing you could say to Bonnie that would cause her to have anything but good words for "her kids"!

Bonnie has faced serious health challenges, and she's unable to help at the church anymore. She misses the children, but it doesn't stop her from serving! She'll send cards to anyone she hears is sick or discouraged—in addition to the birthday cards.

I'm curious to know just how many encouragement-filled envelopes have been sent from Bonnie's address over the years! Looking at my own life, I wonder what I could possibly do that could impact as many people with the love of Jesus as Bonnie does from her small living room. And then I realize *it doesn't matter*. Bonnie never intended her "ministry" to become so far-reaching! She was simply loving others, and her ministry grew.

You know, I think it's time to get some stamps for Mrs. Bonnie...

I love that shirt!

Rock star!

"YOUR LOVE FOR ONE ANOTHER WILL PROVE TO THE WORLD THAT YOU ARE MY DISCIPLES."

You're really great at that!

Way to go!

Terrific!

I can always count on you!

—John 13:35

Keep it up!

THE POWER OF ENCOURAGING WORDS

Great job! *You've got this!* *Mad skills!*

You rock! *Fantastic!*

You shine!

Mr. Slaughter was the most enthusiastic and positive adult I knew in my church's fourth-grade midweek program. I always counted on his goofy yet sincere grin, his clapping hands, and his tireless encouragement: "Great job, Keith!" "You can do it!" "Fantastic!"

Whether I was competing on a sports field or in the classroom, Mr. Slaughter communicated both verbally and with nonverbal expressions that I was important; that to him my efforts mattered greatly.

I don't remember whether I placed first or last in those competitions, but I still remember the power of those encouraging words.

First Thessalonians 5:11 says: "So encourage each other and build each other up, just as you are already doing." To encourage means to "inspire with courage"—to give a can-do feeling. Every word of encouragement you speak to a child is a gift. Be generous with your encouragement—it will go a long way in touching the heart of a child!

Well done! *Hang in there!* *Awesome!*

9

ABOVE
AND BEYOND

We were new to the church, and as a child I was reluctant to get involved. The children's ministry director, Karin, knew this and went out of her way to invite me to play a special role in the Christmas musical. My family was thrilled for me!

Karin arranged to pick me up after school, and together we'd run through lines and practice songs at the church office.

Then came the big performance. I felt special, included, no longer an outsider in a big church. Karin had gone above and beyond for me, and I would never be the same again.

Everyone longs to belong. Ask yourself, *Which children in my ministry need my focus this week?* **How can I help them feel they belong?**

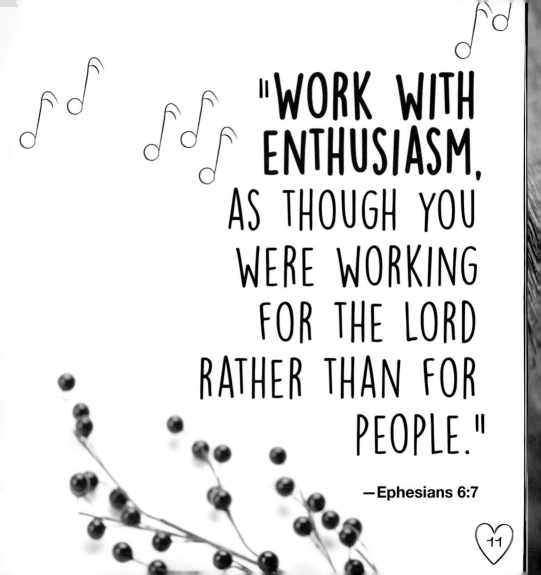

I ASKED A PRESCHOOLER, "WHAT ARE YOU THANKFUL FOR?" HE SAID, "I DON'T KNOW WHAT THANKFUL IS, BUT I KNOW 'THANK FULL' IS BETTER THAN 'THANK EMPTY.'"

—Sheila Halasz

THE SERVANT'S HEART

"FOR EVEN THE SON OF MAN CAME NOT TO BE SERVED BUT TO SERVE OTHERS AND TO GIVE HIS LIFE AS A RANSOM FOR MANY."

—Mark 10:45

My family of five took a mission trip with several other families from our church when I was a teenager. We all piled into a bright-pink charter bus and drove 14 long hours from Colorado to Juarez, Mexico. Once there, we spent a week on the dusty, overcrowded city streets and spread Jesus' love by passing out Bibles, food, and basic living amenities.

The local families who also traveled with us took care of our needs and served us food and water that wouldn't make us sick. But just two days before the end of our trip, my little sister, who was 9 years old at the time, fell extremely ill.

That day was our biggest day of the trip. Our group was tasked with holding a vacation Bible school at a church for extremely poor families living in a *colonia* more than an hour and a half out of town. There were no stops on the drive through the sweltering desert. We piled our supplies into the bus, praying my sister's condition would improve.

It didn't.

After hours of vomiting, her body quickly weakened from dehydration and a rising fever. My worried parents stayed on the bus with her since it was the only place with air conditioning. The rest of us set up the VBS. Meanwhile, hundreds of people were walking along the dirt roads to participate in our event. They were eager to see what the Americans were doing in their secluded neighborhood, where each house was composed of nothing more than a few wood slabs, tarps, bricks, and a square concrete foundation.

15

The tiny church lot was packed with people, and the VBS was going successfully. Children's happy screams of laughter could be heard in all directions. The pastor of the church was ecstatic to see so many people there to learn about Jesus. In the midst of the exciting mayhem, he heard about my sick sister.

Immediately he asked for her to be brought to him. There was nowhere to lay her, so my parents gingerly laid her on the dirty concrete floor. The pastor and his wife placed their hands on her and prayed loudly to God. The pastor was relentless, asking the Lord to heal my sister, a stranger he had just met. His town was completely desolate, unhealthy, and poor, yet he was asking for the healing of one small person.

The virus had left my sister's body by the time we drove home, but the healing Spanish words of the pastor remained with my family. We were there to serve him and his town, yet he immediately stepped in to serve us. The love of God shined through him strongly during those moments of prayer. In a remote town that few will ever see, he stood taller and brighter than many people I will ever meet. It was the perfect reminder that Jesus has no geographical boundaries—his love is endless and his servants are ready to pass it on.

THE PINE  CONE

The doctor's words

rang in my ears: "Positive biopsy…immediate surgery… mastectomy." Crying, I almost didn't see the pine cone in the parking lot.

Suddenly I was a teenager again, sitting near a campfire at church camp.

Our counselor was holding up a pine cone and explaining that it contained seeds we couldn't see — only during the heat of a forest fire would the seeds pop out. But from the ashes, the seeds would sprout, flourish, and mature into sturdy new trees.

God, our counselor said, had likewise given us inner strength to grow again after devastating life events. The pine cone at my feet brought back her words — with God's help, I, too, could grow again.

"BUT THOSE WHO TRUST IN THE LORD WILL FIND NEW STRENGTH. THEY WILL SOAR HIGH ON WINGS LIKE EAGLES. THEY WILL RUN AND NOT GROW WEARY. THEY WILL WALK AND NOT FAINT."

—Isaiah 40:31

19

"THEN JESUS WENT INTO A HOUSE TO GET AWAY FROM THE CROWD."

—Mark 7:17

"JESUS WENT AWAY AND WAS HIDDEN FROM THEM."

—John 12:36

"THEN JESUS LEFT THEM AGAIN AND PRAYED THE SAME PRAYER AS BEFORE."

—Mark 14:39

JUST GET AWAY

Have you noticed that Jesus spent much of his ministry by himself? Of course, he led and counseled the disciples, he performed miracles, and he spoke to crowds. He also needed time to just get away, which, I have to admit, makes me feel so much better. There were times he went away to pray, and there were times he was just done. Other times we're not told what he did, and I find myself guessing. Did he let off steam by working with his hands? Did he have a hobby? Did he go for a walk? Did he have the coveted treat of an afternoon nap?

Just as Jesus did, find time to just get away…in a good way.

Schedule a retreat day. Yes, with just a bit of planning, this can really happen. Take a day off work. If you have children at home, ask a friend to watch them. (You can return the favor later.) The point is to get out of your normal routine and spend some time—just you and God (and a good cup of coffee). Talk to him. Listen to him. Enjoy being with him.

21

Go for a walk. Now, there are times a good walk at the mall is in order, but I'm talking more about getting away into nature. If you don't live near nature, take a different route than you normally do. What do you see? What do you hear? What are you enjoying at this moment?

If you can't make a full day work, at least take a two-minute time-out. In the middle of a stressful day, lock yourself in the bathroom (although I prefer the pantry—it has snacks). Think of something for which you're thankful—really thankful—and breathe. Then put the cheese puffs away, wipe your hands on your jeans, and rejoin your normal life.

Jesus didn't model an exact time table. It doesn't matter how long (or short) your time away may be. Just get away.

"TEACHERS CAN CHANGE LIVES WITH JUST THE RIGHT MIX OF CHALK AND CHALLENGES."

—Joyce Meyer

TAKING GOD'S L🌐VE TO THE WORLD

My fourth-grade teacher

once did a series on the foreign missionaries our church supported. We learned about the countries where they served, the people they ministered to, and the languages, foods, and spiritual beliefs of those people.

She even made a peanut soup from Indonesia that we ate with our fingers as we sat on the floor!

From then on, we began to personally connect to our missionaries in ways we never had before. We better understood who we were praying for, where they were, and what struggles they were facing. And later, three classmates went on mission trips themselves.

Matthew 28:19-20 says, "Therefore, go and make disciples of all the nations, baptizing them in the name of the Father and the Son and the Holy Spirit. Teach these new disciples to obey all the commands I have given you. And be sure of this: I am with you always, even to the end of the age."

As you serve in children's ministry you are making disciples, and you also have the opportunity to help children "go" and make a difference as well!

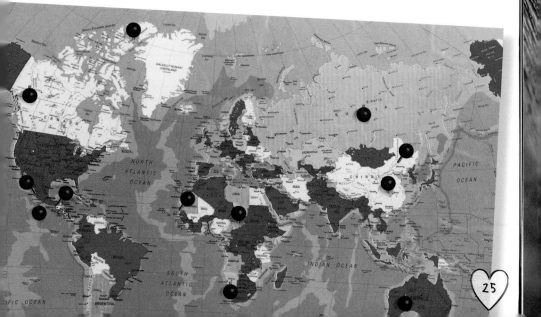

SPECIAL TALENTS

Stuart was a professional guitar player who assisted in our church's youth group. He soon discovered which of us students were interested in music and invited us to play our instruments as he led the singing.

Eventually Stuart asked me to play piano in a Christian band he had started, and in college, I began leading worship on my own for various groups and churches.

Stuart was the first person to invite me to use my musical talents to help others. Today I coach worship leaders all over the country and help churches renew and revitalize their worship services.

BUTTING IN

A few years ago,

our family was driving across town to go ice skating as snow fell heavily. Realizing the roads were worse than we had thought, my husband and I began to consider turning back and trying again on a clearer day. Just as protests from the kids began to erupt, we heard one of our daughters, who was 10 at the time, tell her twin sister in her most mature voice, "Let's be quiet until they make their decision; then we'll butt in."

I've felt the same way many times. I know God is always faithful to fulfill his promises, but it seems that when life gets stormy, I despair. Just like my daughter, I start off with mature prayers and platitudes, but in a corner of my heart "butting in" is my backup plan. As the storm continues and I feel as if God's promises aren't being fulfilled, I begin to butt in. I lie awake at night and tell him in great detail exactly how I think things should go moving forward. I beg and plead and cajole. I worry about what will happen if things don't go my way.

The great thing about God, though, is that the fulfillment of his promises doesn't hinge on my maturity—or my lack thereof. I am precious and loved by him, regardless of whether I'm praying in my mature voice or I'm "butting in." He keeps me in his tender care. When the time is right, and despite the storms, his promises will faithfully be fulfilled. He will calm my heart and quiet my fears. I am in his hands—and so are you.

"I'D HAVE TO SAY I'M MOST PROUD OF MY MENTORING CAMP THAT I DO IN DALLAS EVERY YEAR FOR ONE HUNDRED BOYS FROM SINGLE–PARENT HOMES. I WAS RAISED BY A MOTHER WHO WAS A SUNDAY SCHOOL TEACHER AND A FATHER WHO WORKED HARD. TOGETHER THEY TAUGHT ME TO GIVE BACK."

—Steve Harvey

29

≫ PASS IT ON ≫

For years I struggled with receiving kindness from others—not out of ungratefulness, but rather from guilt because I couldn't always repay the kindness.

When friends stepped in to help while our youngest daughter was in the hospital, I fretted, "I'll never be able to repay you."

"Don't worry," one friend said. "I'm just passing on help I've received."

She told me about hearing the story of the good Samaritan in Sunday school. The man on the road to Jericho couldn't repay the Samaritan, her teacher had explained, so he passed on that kindness to another.

My friend was remembering the lesson she'd learned long ago and passing it on to me. Now I remember the lesson and pass it on, too.

"NOW WHICH OF THESE THREE WOULD YOU SAY WAS A NEIGHBOR TO THE MAN WHO WAS ATTACKED BY BANDITS?" JESUS ASKED.

THE MAN REPLIED, "THE ONE WHO SHOWED HIM MERCY."

THEN JESUS SAID, "YES, NOW GO AND DO THE SAME."

—Luke 10:36-37

"SHOUT WITH JOY TO THE LORD, ALL THE EARTH! WORSHIP THE LORD WITH GLADNESS. COME BEFORE HIM, SINGING WITH JOY."

—Psalm 100:1-2

PRAISE WITH GUSTO

Frank filled many roles in my life, from Sunday school teacher in junior high to confirmation mentor to great personal friend. But his greatest influence on me was as a member of the adult choir.

In church, my family always sat close to the front where we had a good view of the choir. As soon as the first note of any song sounded, Frank's face would break into a huge grin, and he would begin to worship. He praised God with gusto!

Every time I watched Frank sing, I wanted to praise God, too.

34

"GRATITUDE MAKES SENSE OF OUR PAST, BRINGS PEACE FOR TODAY, AND CREATES A VISION FOR TOMORROW."

—Melody Beattie

A FAMILY AFFAIR

I was cast— "casted" might be a more accurate word—into children's ministry at an early age.

One evening my parents brought the whole family along to paint a room that would be used for children's church. While they worked, my brother and I, one room over, built a tower of chairs atop a table. I climbed on top. And like the walls of Jericho, my tower and I came tumbling down!

My parents rushed me to the ER, and my elbow was reset. I wore a cast for weeks. I barely remember the pain from that incident, but I do remember the fact that my parents had grabbed a paintbrush and gotten involved to help make children's church a great place to be—for my sake.

> *"...I do remember the fact that my parents had grabbed a paintbrush and gotten involved..."*

"THE LORD IS OUR GOD, THE LORD ALONE. AND YOU MUST LOVE THE LORD YOUR GOD WITH ALL YOUR HEART, ALL YOUR SOUL, AND ALL YOUR STRENGTH. AND YOU MUST COMMIT YOURSELVES WHOLEHEARTEDLY TO THESE COMMANDS THAT I AM GIVING YOU TODAY. REPEAT THEM AGAIN AND AGAIN TO YOUR CHILDREN."

—Deuteronomy 6:4-6

A CATCHY TUNE

My parents were probably annoyed that I sang "Matthew, Mark, Luke, and John..." to the tune of "Yankee Doodle" over and over, day in and day out.

But it wasn't my fault!

My Sunday school teacher was to blame. She taught our class the books of the New Testament in canonical order using that catchy tune. We'd sing it each week. The result? The song—and the names of the New Testament books—became forever embedded in my brain.

Decades later, I still sometimes burst out in song during Bible study or quietly whisper the song while looking up a certain verse. My teacher made learning fun by using a creative mnemonic device—singing—and the learning stuck!

Isaiah	Romans
Jeremiah	1 Corinthians
Lamentations	2 Corinthians
Ezekiel	Galatians
...omy Daniel	Ephesians
Hosea	Philippians
Joel	Colossians
Amos	1 Thessalonians
...el Obadiah	2 Thessalonians
...uel Jonah	1 Timothy
...s Micah	2 Timothy
...gs Nahum	Titus
...onicles Habakkuk	Philemon
...ronicles Zephaniah	Hebrews
Haggai	James
...miah Zechariah	1 Peter
...er Malachi	2 Peter
Matthew	1 John
...lms Mark	2 John
...overbs Luke	3 John
...clesiastes John	Jude
...ng of Songs Acts	Revelation

"MAY THE WORDS OF MY MOUTH AND THE MEDITATION OF MY HEART BE PLEASING TO YOU, O LORD, MY ROCK AND MY REDEEMER."

—Psalm 19:14

39

"JESUS LOVES THE LITTLE CHILDREN— ALL THE CHILDREN OF THE ."

THE MOST EXCELLENT WAY

Every year our elementary Sunday school classes would put together care packages filled with fun, practical things for the church's college students. We'd include gum, ramen noodles, gift certificates, coffee, and toothpaste.

We had fun and got excited about college—and the day we would get our own care packages!

Our teachers, whether shopping for the goodies, finding mailing boxes, looking up addresses, or keeping us fed with pizza, did everything in the most excellent way. It wasn't just a job to them. At some time along the way, they had taught most of the college students these boxes were intended for…and they still cared deeply for them.

That's how I knew that my teachers would always care for me, too.

APPLE PIE ORDER

One evening, frustration toward a co-worker— and an unrelated request for apple pie—brought to mind a summer Bible school lesson from my childhood.

Mrs. Bertodi had brought apples from her tree. They were covered with a foggy film, and she polished them one by one as she spoke.

"People are like apples. You can't always trust that what you see on the outside is what's really on the inside." She placed an apple on its side and sliced through it. Then she held up one half and pointed out the seeded star right in the center. "God wants us to look inside to see the good in others," she told us.

Now, as I prepared the pie, I cut an apple in half. There was the star! I vowed to look for the good in my co-worker.

"LET MY TEACHING FALL ON YOU LIKE RAIN; LET MY SPEECH SETTLE LIKE DEW. LET MY WORDS FALL LIKE RAIN ON TENDER GRASS, LIKE GENTLE SHOWERS ON YOUNG PLANTS."

—Deuteronomy 32:2

UNCONDITIONAL L♥VE

My earliest memories
of Sunday school include my teacher Miss Huisjen.

I think I fell in love with Jesus partly because of her kindness in showing me Jesus' love. (Years later, I volunteered to teach a Sunday school kindergarten class so that I, too, could share Jesus' love with children.)

One Christmas, Miss Huisjen gave me a small ring made of copper with a pink enamel coating. On the band was a picture of a dove carrying an olive branch. The gift was probably inexpensive, but to a child it was priceless.

I looked for the ring today. It appears as though the ring and I have become separated.

But I am confident that nothing can ever separate me from the love of God in Jesus Christ.

"AND I AM CONVINCED THAT NOTHING CAN EVER SEPARATE US FROM GOD'S LOVE. NEITHER DEATH NOR LIFE, NEITHER ANGELS NOR DEMONS, NEITHER OUR FEARS FOR TODAY NOR OUR WORRIES ABOUT TOMORROW—NOT EVEN THE POWERS OF HELL CAN SEPARATE US FROM GOD'S LOVE. NO POWER IN THE SKY ABOVE OR IN THE EARTH BELOW—INDEED, NOTHING IN ALL CREATION WILL EVER BE ABLE TO SEPARATE US FROM THE LOVE OF GOD THAT IS REVEALED IN CHRIST JESUS OUR LORD."

—Romans 8:38-39

45

AS IMPORTANT AS GOOD CURRICULUM AND WELL-PLANNED LESSONS ARE, CHILDREN WILL MOST LIKELY REMEMBER HOW YOU MADE THEM FEEL.

HOW DO THE KIDS IN YOUR LIFE FEEL GOD'S UNCONDITIONAL LOVE THROUGH YOU?

SWEET VOICES

As I slid into the pew, I was still reeling from the dreaded pink slip I'd received. It wasn't fair!

Organ music interrupted my thoughts. The children's choir filed in, and their sweet voices transported me back to the time I sang in children's choir. Our director always reminded us to think about the words we sang.

Suddenly one of the songs he'd taught us popped into my mind: "Jesus… has a plan for your life, and you know he'll always be there."

In the months that followed, I often hummed that tune. Changes did come, but God had a plan for my life. He would always be there.

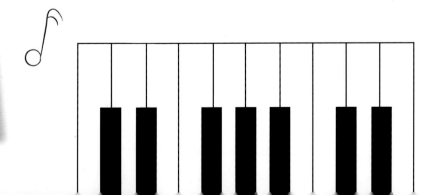

47

FROM MUNDANE TO MEANINGFUL

I was fresh out of Bible college and ready to change the world as I began work in my first congregation. It was there that I met Alma.

Alma was 85 years old and had served as the Sunday school secretary for 25 years. Every Sunday she collected the offering baskets and attendance records from each classroom. Then she sat patiently in the office, updating each student's attendance record and counting the donations.

Twenty-five years in this one volunteer position? Really?

"Alma, what keeps you motivated to do this task?" I finally asked her one day. (It was the last thing I'd be willing to do, since I didn't see any eternal significance in the tasks, and frankly, I thought it was rather… well, boring.)

She looked at me and said, "Oh, I'm not just taking attendance. Every time I put a check mark next to the students' names, I pray for each child. I ask God to be with them, their families, and help them grow closer to God."

At that moment, I felt like crawling under a rock.

Alma was motivated to serve in this position (for 25 years!) because she saw the greater good. She took a task and turned it into a ministry. She taught me a valuable lesson: Everything we do for the kingdom matters, no matter how mundane or insignificant it may seem—because people matter to God.

Two months later I visited a fourth-grade Sunday school student named Jessica who had just been hospitalized for a ruptured appendix. Her parents were anxious, but Jessica remained calm and optimistic. We prayed before her surgery, and I told her not to worry because God would take care of her.

She replied, "I know, because Miss Alma told me she prays for me each week in Sunday school."

I still think of Alma today as I see church volunteers handing out worship bulletins, changing dirty diapers in the nursery, serving refreshments, and taking care of a hundred other tasks that need to be accomplished so we can live out our call to be the church. Alma used her gift of intercession to add significance to the task of taking attendance. She knew what it meant to "pray at all times and on every occasion" (Ephesians 6:18). Even the occasion of placing check marks next to names on a class roster.

What daily tasks has God called you to do? Take the kids to their soccer game? Cut the lawn? Walk the dog? Because of Alma, I'm challenged to connect the mundane to mission, the earthly chore to the heavenly outcome—even if that means taking out the trash. *Thank you, Alma!*

I CAN DO IT!

Mrs. Ussery was young, pretty—and new. She didn't do things the way our other Sunday school teachers did them.

She asked who wanted to read—she didn't assign verses. She let us create crafts out of strings, edible glitter (!), mint-flavored paste, and feathers. And she didn't hold up samples of finished crafts that I could never quite replicate.

Mrs. Ussery let us be creative. By allowing us to make choices, she taught us the power of initiative.

Because of her, I have never stopped learning!

50

"PERSONALLY I'M ALWAYS READY TO LEARN, ALTHOUGH I DO NOT ALWAYS LIKE BEING TAUGHT."

—Winston Churchill

A WISE SUGGESTION

I was young when my family moved. Lacking enthusiasm for an unfamiliar place of worship, my family attended church sporadically.

I noticed that several children in my third-grade Sunday school class had new, red Bibles—gifts for Promotion Sunday. I asked if I could have one.

The teacher, reading my hesitation to commit, wisely suggested that I earn a Bible by attending class three weeks in a row.

I influenced my family to attend consistently, received the Bible, and committed to what eventually became my middle school and high school youth group.

HOLY BIBLE

SAY IT
LOUDER
NOW!

I'm not exactly a brave person. In fact, being a worrier is what I'm known for among my friends and family. They always seem quite amused at whatever my latest worry is. For example, a huge fear of mine at the moment is being attacked by bats while I sleep. I grew up in a house with bats in the attic…so I'm sure it isn't exactly out of the realm of possibility.

All jokes aside, fear and worry are the biggest struggles for me in my Christian walk. Worry over life at the moment, worry for the future, worry about when I'm supposed to step out in faith, worry if I'm following God as he is leading me or not. I *know* I am to trust God and that he will protect me. It's his promise. But it's still not easy for me.

One of the roles I've been blessed with over the years is being a Sunday school teacher to preschoolers. In a recent lesson, the children were memorizing Joshua 1:9. In my lesson prep, the actual words of the verse didn't really stand out to me.

On that Sunday morning, I was struck at the irony of *me* teaching about trusting God. We practiced saying the words to the verse and added in some fun hand motions. We started by saying the verse as softly as we could, and then we gradually grew louder as I shouted, "Say it louder now!"

I was brought to tears as I watched Kenzie, Mason, Cameron, Jaxon, and the rest of their 3-year-old classmates shout as loudly as they could how God is with them all the time. Later when we were discussing the different circumstances in which God is with us, I had quite a chuckle listening to their examples (you can use your imagination!).

In that moment for those 3-year-olds, the thought of God being everywhere was enough. It filled them with joy and excitement. They weren't asking questions or doubting. God is the friend who doesn't have to leave and go home.

As I was cleaning up the crushed Cheerios on the floor, I realized I should have the same exuberance over God's presence in my life. I truly don't have to fear—because he is with me always.

God puts all kinds of people in our lives to inspire us and remind us of what's important. That Sunday, those fifteen 3-year-olds spoke more truth into my life than they could have ever realized. They reminded me it's okay to trust God without hesitation or fear.

"THIS IS MY COMMAND—BE STRONG AND COURAGEOUS! DO NOT BE AFRAID OR DISCOURAGED. FOR THE LORD YOUR GOD IS WITH YOU WHEREVER YOU GO."

—Joshua 1:9

SEEING THE FUTURE ME

"I see such a precious spirit within you for loving God…I'll always know that somewhere you're singing and sharing Jesus."

Miss Pat wrote these words in the back of the hymnal she gave me when I "graduated" from children's choir. In her letter, Miss Pat spoke a vision into my life. She instilled in me a sense of future—a future of strong, unshakable faith in Christ. She ministered to me as a kid, all the while praying and hoping for the adult I would someday become.

Miss Pat saw the future me—and helped me see it, too.

Ask yourself, *How can I speak vision into the life of a child?*

Write a letter (perhaps as part of a keepsake) describing the child's positive traits and the strong faith you hope he or she will have as an adult.

57

"TEACH ME YOUR DECREES, O LORD; I WILL KEEP THEM TO THE END. GIVE ME UNDERSTANDING AND I WILL OBEY YOUR INSTRUCTIONS; I WILL PUT THEM INTO PRACTICE WITH ALL MY HEART. MAKE ME WALK ALONG THE PATH OF YOUR COMMANDS, FOR THAT IS WHERE MY HAPPINESS IS FOUND."

—Psalm 119:33-35

KEEP IT SIMPLE

I watched the animated movie *Brave* with many of my family members. If you haven't seen it, it's the story of a Scottish princess who (we are told at the beginning) wants to change her fate. When the movie ended, I asked my nephew, Will, who's 8, what he thought of the movie. He reacted with a bit of disappointment.

"I kept waiting, but she never changed her feet!"

Mix together the heavy Scottish accents and the fact that "fate" is an abstract concept for children, and Will had gotten the idea early on in the movie that the princess would change her feet!

It's easy to laugh at the funny things kids say and how they can get the wrong idea from misunderstanding things that seem simple to adults. But I wonder how many times I've had the wrong idea. I've heard something that was never said, or I've been looking down one road when I should have been walking down another. Life is confusing, and it's easy to get distracted or miss the point. That's why I'm thankful for simple portions of the Bible that make it easy to get refocused.

Micah 6:8 says, "O people, the Lord has told you what is good, and this is what he requires of you: to do what is right, to love mercy, and to walk humbly with your God."

Do right.

Love mercy.

Walk humbly with God.

It's that simple.

SMILE!

May God be merciful and bless us.

May his face smile with favor on us.

May your ways be known throughout the earth, your saving power among people everywhere. May the nations praise you, O God. Yes, may all the nations praise you.

Let the whole world sing for joy, because you govern the nations with justice and guide the people of the whole world.

May the nations praise you, O God. Yes, may all the nations praise you.

Then the earth will yield its harvests, and God, our God, will richly bless us.

Yes, God will bless us, and people all over the world will fear him

(Psalm 67).

May God smile with favor on you today! And remember to share your own smile with someone else!